Learning to read. Reading to learn!

LEVEL ONE Sounding It Out Preschool–Kindergarten
For kids who know their alphabet and are starting to sound out words.

learning sight words • beginning reading • sounding out words

LEVEL TWO Reading with Help Preschool–Grade 1
For kids who know sight words and are learning to sound out new words.

expanding vocabulary • building confidence • sounding out bigger words

LEVEL THREE Independent Reading Grades 1–3
For kids who are beginning to read on their own.

introducing paragraphs • challenging vocabulary • reading for comprehension

LEVEL FOUR Chapters Grades 2–4
For confident readers who enjoy a mixture of images and story.

reading for learning • more complex content • feeding curiosity

Ripley Readers Designed to help kids build their reading skills and confidence at any level, this program offers a variety of fun, entertaining, and unbelievable topics to interest even the most reluctant readers. With stories and information that will spark their curiosity, each book will motivate them to start and keep reading.

Vice President, Licensing & Publishing Amanda Joiner
Editorial Manager Carrie Bolin

Editor Jordie R. Orlando
Writer Korynn Wible-Freels
Designer Rose Audette
Reprographics Bob Prohaska

Published by Ripley Publishing 2020

10 9 8 7 6 5 4 3 2 1

Copyright © 2020 Ripley Publishing

ISBN: 978-1-60991-453-0

For more information regarding permission, contact:
VP Licensing & Publishing
Ripley Entertainment Inc.
7576 Kingspointe Parkway, Suite 188
Orlando, Florida 32819

Email: publishing@ripleys.com
www.ripleys.com/books
Manufactured in China in January 2020.

First Printing

Library of Congress Control Number: 2019942269

PUBLISHER'S NOTE
While every effort has been made to verify the accuracy of the entries in this book, the Publisher cannot be held responsible for any errors contained in the work. They would be glad to receive any information from readers.

PHOTO CREDITS
Cover, 3, 18–19 metha1819/Shutterstock.com; **Master Graphics** © VectorShots/Shutterstock.com, © Gluiki/Shutterstock.com; **4–5** © SAHACHATZ/Shutterstock.com; **6–7** © AmeliAU/Shutterstock.com; **7** (c), **36** (b) © Mark_Kostich/Shutterstock.com; **8, 15** (br) © paleontologist natural/Shutterstock.com; **9** © Rose3663/Shutterstock.com; **10** (t) © Miceking/Shutterstock.com, (b) © Svetsol/Shutterstock.com; **10** (c), **17** (cl) © Kozyreva Elena/Shutterstock.com; **11** © AKKHARAT JARUSILAWONG/Shutterstock.com; **12–13** (dps) © Marcio Jose Bastos Silva/Shutterstock.com; **12** (bl) © Alex Coan/Shutterstock.com; **14–15** © frantic00/Shutterstock.com; **15** © Minohek/Shutterstock.com; **16** © netsuthep/Shutterstock.com; **17** (t) © Jaroslav Moravcik/Shutterstock.com; **20–21** (dps) **21** (t), **32–33, 35** (br), **40–41, 46** (br), **47** (cl) © Daniel Eskridge/Shutterstock.com; **22–23** (dps) © Michael Rosskothen/Shutterstock.com; **23** (c) © AkimD/Shutterstock.com; **24–25** Science Photo Library/Alamy Stock Photo; **26-27** © Elenarts/Shutterstock.com; **28–29** MasPix/Alamy Stock Photo; **30–31, 44–45, 47** (tr) © Herschel Hoffmeyer/Shutterstock.com; **34–35, 35** (tr), **36** (t) © Warpaint/Shutterstock.com; **37, 43** © Catmando/Shutterstock.com; **38–39, 46** (tl) © solarseven/Shutterstock.com; **40** (c) © Eric Isselee/Shutterstock.com, (b) © Svetlana Foote/Shutterstock.com; **42** MAF/Alamy Stock Photo; **46** (tr) © Digital Storm/Shutterstock.com, (bl) © Dotted Yeti/Shutterstock.com; **47** (tl) © Redchanka/Shutterstock.com, (cr) © Elnur/Shutterstock.com, (bl) © Manfred Ruckszio/Shutterstock.com, (br) © Ihor Matsiievskyi/Shutterstock.com

Key: t = top, b = bottom, c = center, l = left, r = right, sp = single page, dp = double page, bkg = background

Ripley Readers

Dinosaurs!

All true and unbelievable!

RIPLEY
PUBLISHING
a Jim Pattison Company

TABLE OF CONTENTS

CHAPTER 1

WHAT IS A DINOSAUR?

Imagine you're digging in a field 200 years ago. You come across a strange rock that looks like a tooth! What animal would have a tooth so big and sharp?

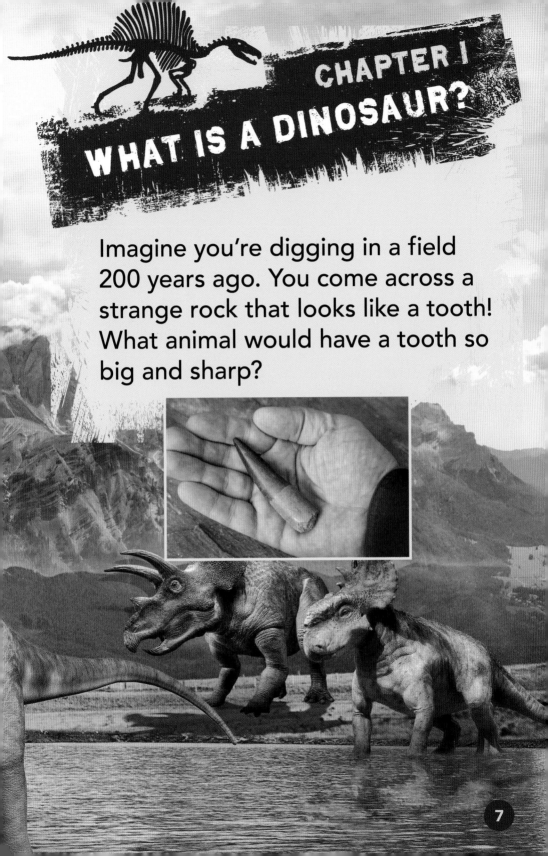

People have been digging up dinosaur bones for thousands of years. A lot of times it happens by accident! Many thought they belonged to other animals or even to giant people.

Scientist Richard Owen chose the name *dinosauria* for these mysterious bones in 1842.

Dinosauria means terrible lizard. Today, **dinosaur** is a word that people know all around the world!

Dinosaurs were reptiles who are now **extinct**. Dinosaurs had legs below their bodies. This is different from other reptiles. Alligators have legs that are out to the side.

You can't go to the zoo to see a dinosaur exhibit. These beasts lived millions of years ago!

Did you know that not all dinosaurs lived at the same time?

Scientists break up the millions of years that dinosaurs lived into three periods:

TRIASSIC PERIOD: the oldest period. A small, sharp-toothed Eoraptor could be found during this time.

JURASSIC PERIOD: the middle period. A long-necked Brachiosaurus was alive in this period.

CRETACEOUS PERIOD: the most recent period. The famous Tyrannosaurus rex was a Cretaceous dinosaur.

Dinosaurs lived millions of years ago. So how do we know so much about them?

Paleontologists study them. These special scientists find and study dinosaur fossils.

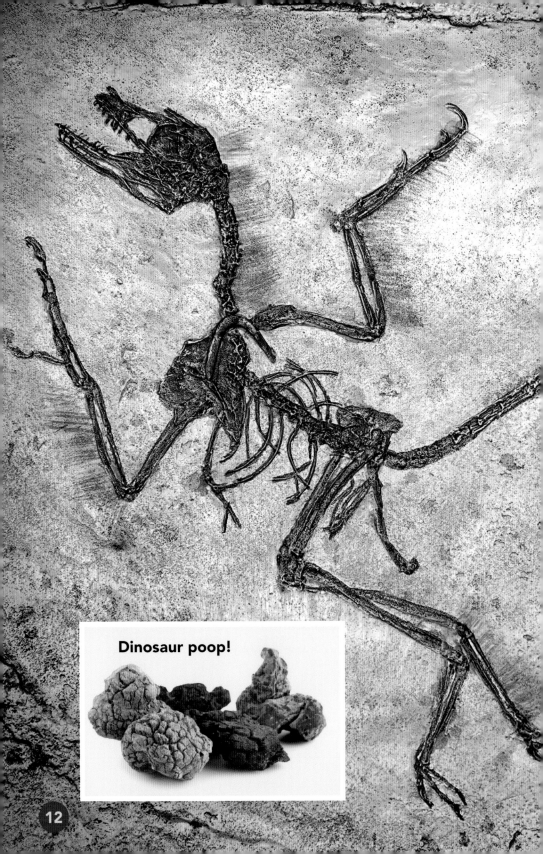

Dinosaur poop!

FOSSILS

A **fossil** is evidence of a living thing from long ago. There are two kinds of fossils: body fossils and trace fossils.

Body fossils are body parts. They are made of things like teeth or bones. Layers of **silt** have protected them in the Earth.

Trace fossils are proof that living things existed. They are things like footprints or even poop! Trace fossils are made when those types of things are covered by **sediment** and then harden.

Fossils are found in very old rock layers all over the world. Scientists say the best places to look for fossils are dry areas without buildings or trees.

Scientists use different tools to help them find and uncover fossils. Fossils are found in rock layers. They are surrounded by hard stone! Chisels are needed to break the rocks. A brush helps clear away the dust.

Tools for digging to find fossils

Footprints and eggs are also trace fossils. Storms uncovered 85 dinosaur footprints in England recently. This was an exciting discovery for scientists!

Believe It or Not... Some dinosaurs could lay 20 eggs at one time!

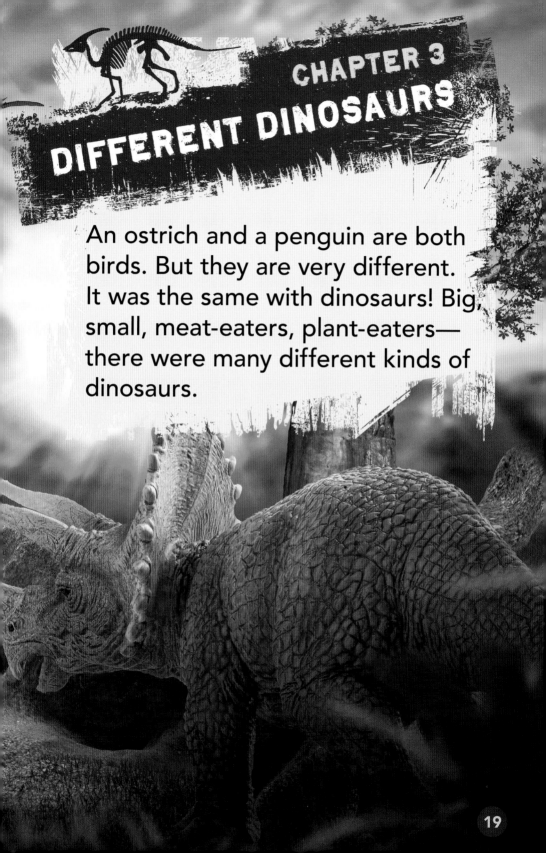

CHAPTER 3
DIFFERENT DINOSAURS

An ostrich and a penguin are both birds. But they are very different. It was the same with dinosaurs! Big, small, meat-eaters, plant-eaters— there were many different kinds of dinosaurs.

Dinosaurs can be put into two groups based on their hip shapes. Some walked on two legs. This is like birds today. Others walked on four legs. They moved around more like lizards.

Some dinosaurs were so big! Imagine a reptile as tall as a six-story building. The large bones of an Argentinosaurus were found in Argentina.

Believe *It* or *Not*... The blue whale is the largest creature that has ever lived.

It is even bigger than dinosaurs! The blue whale is in danger of becoming extinct. It is our job to help keep them safe!

Not all dinosaurs were huge. The Compsognathus was only the size of a chicken!

What was a dinosaur's favorite snack? It depends on the dino!

Plant-eaters were **herbivores**. Meat-eaters were **carnivores**. Dinosaurs who ate plants and meat were **omnivores**.

Did you know the biggest dinosaurs were gentle and only ate plants?

CHAPTER 4
FEROCIOUS FIGHTERS

Animals sometimes get into fights.
They might battle to protect
their babies or to hunt for food.
Dinosaurs got into fights, too.

Lots of dinosaurs were ready to protect themselves with spikes, horns, and armor. This dinosaur even had a club on its tail!

Don't choose a battle with one of these bad boys! Sharp teeth and claws were dangerous weapons.

Which do you think would win a fight? A T. rex with its teeth and claws? Or a Triceratops with its long horns?

CHAPTER 5

NOT QUITE A DINOSAUR

Dinosaurs were not the only creatures living millions of years ago. There were other creatures that were a lot like dinosaurs. But they had some big differences.

Pterosaurs were flying reptiles. They looked a lot like giant birds! They had wings, two legs, and a long mouth shaped like a beak.

There were also reptiles who lived in the water.

Plesiosaurus had four flippers and a long neck.

Kronosaurus looked like an alligator with flippers!

Believe It or Not... Other large animals lived after the age of the dinosaurs. A very big kind of shark roamed the seas! The megalodon lived millions of years ago. Its bite was stronger than a T. rex's!

Megalodon shark tooth fossil

Modern great white shark tooth

CHAPTER 6

WHERE DID THE DINOSAURS GO?

The dinosaurs used to rule the land. So, what happened? Where are they now?

Scientists do not know exactly how the dinosaurs died. Right now, it is believed that a giant **asteroid** hit the Earth.

Fire, floods, rocks, and ash killed most of life on Earth. The dust and soot stayed in the air for months. The sun was blocked out, the rain turned to mud, and the dinosaurs disappeared.

Scientists believe that today's birds evolved from a group of small meat-eating dinosaurs! Their bones, eggs, and behaviors are helpful pieces of evidence.

Believe It or Not... Today's alligators and crocodiles are not dinosaurs. But their ancestors lived during that same time. Their looks have barely changed over millions of years!

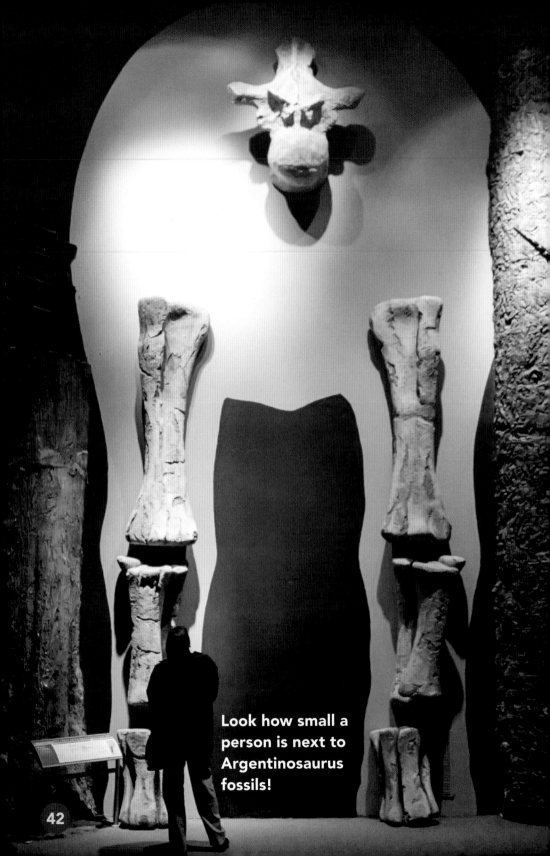

Look how small a person is next to Argentinosaurus fossils!

CHAPTER 7

THE FUTURE OF DINOSAURS

There have been about 700 species of dinosaurs discovered. More are being found all the time. In October 2018, scientists found one of the largest dinosaurs to have ever lived!

A lot of time and research is needed to make sure dinosaur facts are true. There are no live dinosaurs to study. Scientists must study fossils instead.

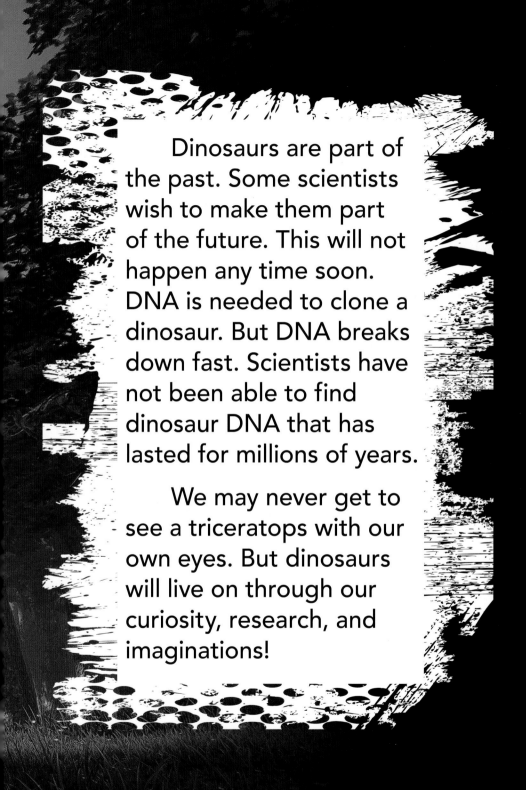

Dinosaurs are part of the past. Some scientists wish to make them part of the future. This will not happen any time soon. DNA is needed to clone a dinosaur. But DNA breaks down fast. Scientists have not been able to find dinosaur DNA that has lasted for millions of years.

We may never get to see a triceratops with our own eyes. But dinosaurs will live on through our curiosity, research, and imaginations!

GLOSSARY

asteroid: one of thousands of rocks found between Mars and Jupiter.

carnivores: animals that eat meat.

dinosaur: largest known land animals from the past.

extinct: something that no longer exists.

fossil: any trace of a living thing from an earlier age (bones, footprints, etc.).

herbivores: animals that eat plants.

omnivores: animals that eat plants and meat.

paleontologist: scientists with a deep knowledge of living things from earlier ages.

silt: loose soil with rock particles.

sediment: material that settles to the bottom of a liquid.

Ready for More?

Ripley Readers feature unbelievable but true facts and stories!

Sharks!

Trucks!

Pets

Shipwrecks

Weather

Horses

Bizarre Buildings

Dinosaurs!

**For more information about
Ripley's Believe It or Not!, go to www.ripleys.com**